EXPLORING COUNTRIES

China

STEVE GOLDSWORTHY

MEDIA ENHANCED BOOKS

AV2 BY WEIGL

ADDED VALUE • AUDIO VISUAL

www.av2books.com

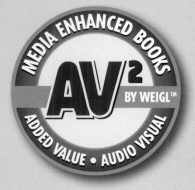

AV² provides enriched content that supplements and complements this book. Weigl's AV² books strive to create inspired learning and engage young minds in a total learning experience.

Your AV² Media Enhanced books come alive with...

Audio
Listen to sections of the book read aloud.

Key Words
Study vocabulary, and complete a matching word activity.

Go to **www.av2books.com**, and enter this book's unique code.

Video
Watch informative video clips.

Quizzes
Test your knowledge.

BOOK CODE

K 7 5 5 1 0 9

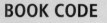

Embedded Weblinks
Gain additional information for research.

Slide Show
View images and captions, and prepare a presentation.

AV² by Weigl brings you media enhanced books that support active learning.

Try This!
Complete activities and hands-on experiments.

... and much, much more!

Published by AV² by Weigl
350 5th Avenue, 59th Floor
New York, NY 10118
Website: www.av2books.com   www.weigl.com

Library of Congress Cataloging-in-Publication Data

Goldsworthy, Steve.
 China / Steve Goldsworthy.
   p. cm. -- (Exploring countries)
Includes index.
ISBN 978-1-62127-252-6 (hardcover : alk. paper) -- ISBN 978-1-62127-258-8 (softcover : alk. paper)
1. China--Juvenile literature. I. Title.
DS706.G458 2013
951--dc23
                    2012041279

Printed in the United States of America in North Mankato, Minnesota
1 2 3 4 5 6 7 8 9 0 17 16 15 14 13
052013
WEP040413

Editor Jason McClure
Art Director Terry Paulhus

Photo Credits
Every reasonable effort has been made to trace ownership and to obtain permission to reprint copyright material. The publishers would be pleased to have any errors or omissions brought to their attention so that they may be corrected in subsequent printings.

Weigl acknowledges Getty Images as its primary image supplier for this title.

Contents

AV² Book Code......................2

China Overview.................. 4

Exploring China 6

Land and Climate......................8

Plants and Animals 10

Natural Resources...................... 11

Tourism...................... 12

Industry 14

Goods and Services...................... 15

Indigenous Peoples...................... 16

The Age of Exploration 17

Early Settlers...................... 18

Population 20

Politics and Government.............21

Cultural Groups 22

Arts and Entertainment...............24

Sports 26

Mapping China......................28

Quiz Time...................... 30

Key Words 31

Index 31

Log on to av2books.com..............32

China Overview

China is a vast country with a wide variety of landscapes and climates. Located on the continent of Asia, it is a land of deserts and tropical forests, of great rivers and plains. China is home to some of the world's tallest mountains. As diverse as the land is, so are the people that inhabit it. The most populated country in the world, China has an amazing blend of the traditional and modern.

China is home to several endangered animals, including the giant panda. It is estimated that there are only 1,600 giant pandas living in nature in the world.

Most Chinese live in urban areas. They live in cities, with the most up-to-date technologies.

Many Chinese live simple lives, farming in much the same way as their ancestors did.

Temples dot the Chinese landscape, providing a link to the country's history.

The Chinese are an active people. Many of the world's best-known martial arts originated in China.

Exploring *China*

With an area of almost 3.7 million square miles (9.6 million sq. kilometers), China is fourth largest country in the world. Only Russia, the United States, and Canada are larger. China is a diverse land, with a varied geography. Deserts, rivers, and **plateaus** are just some of the country's geographical features.

Tibetan Plateau

Pakistan

N

India

C H

Tibetan Plateau

Yangtze River

Burma

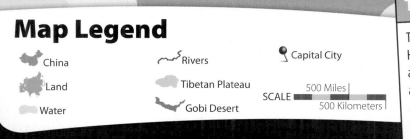

Map Legend

- China
- Land
- Water
- Rivers
- Tibetan Plateau
- Gobi Desert
- Capital City

SCALE
500 Miles
500 Kilometers

Tibetan Plateau

The Tibetan Plateau is located in the Himalayan region of China. Also known as the "Roof of the World," it is the highest and largest plateau on Earth. It covers almost 1 million square miles (2.6 million sq. km). That is about four times the size of the state of Texas.

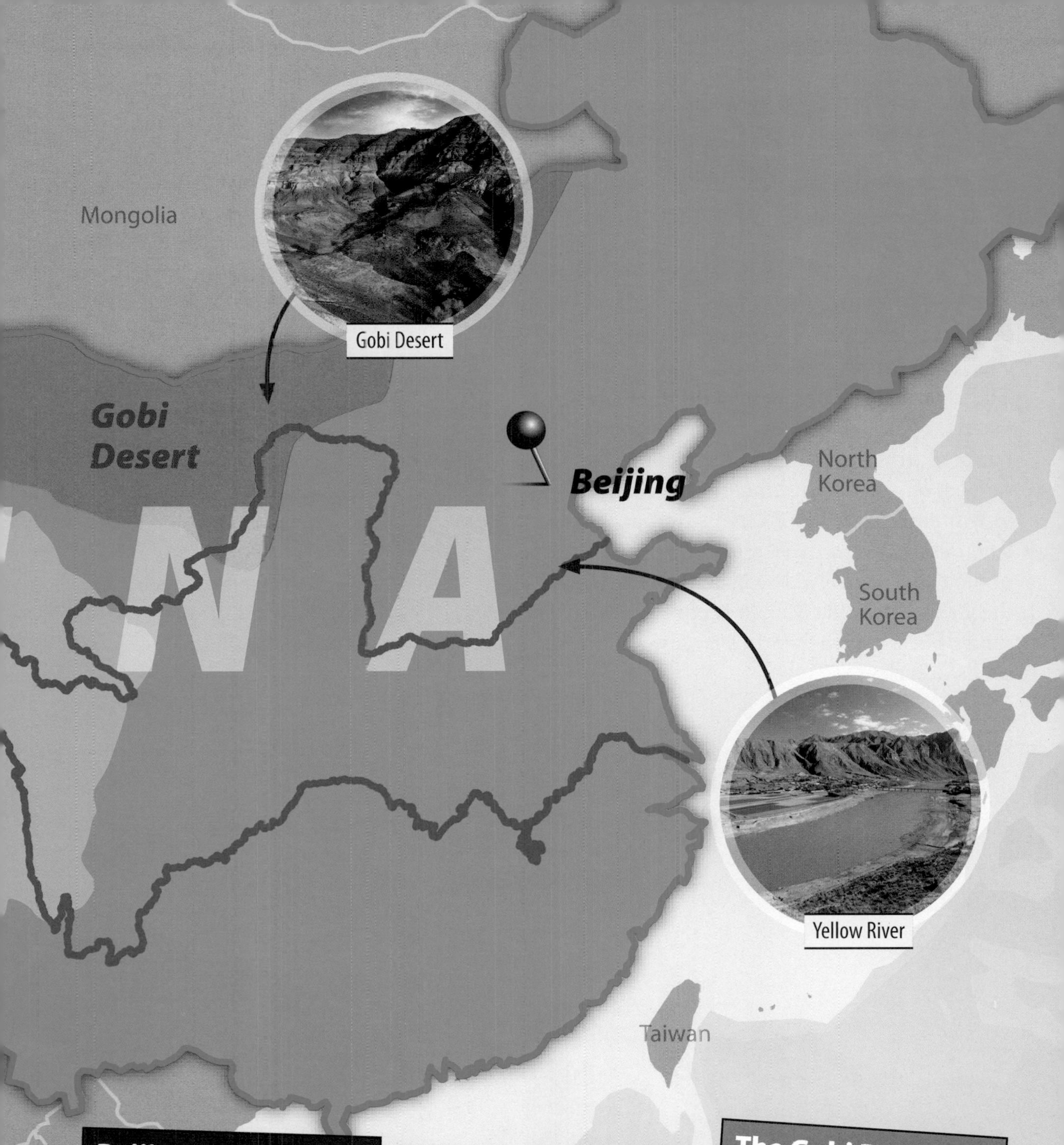

Mongolia

Gobi Desert

Gobi Desert

North Korea

Beijing

South Korea

Yellow River

Taiwan

Beijing

Beijing is the capital city of China. Located in northern China, it is the country's political, economic, and cultural center. Beijing has a population of about 20 million, making it one of the most populous cities in the world.

Yangtze and Yellow Rivers

The Yangtze River and the Yellow River are two of China's most important rivers. The Yangtze River is the longest river in Asia and the third longest in the world.

The Gobi Desert

The Gobi Desert is the largest desert in Asia. It stretches about 500,000 square miles (1,300,000 sq. km) through China and Mongolia. While the Gobi Desert has a barren landscape, it is not sandy. It is composed mainly of bare rock.

LAND AND CLIMATE

Grasslands cover a large area of northern China. This sparse, dry region is made up of tall grasses and small shrubs. These grasslands stretch around the Gobi Desert. High winds contribute to extreme temperatures in the Gobi Desert. They can range from –40° Fahrenheit (–40° Celsius) in winter to 122° F (50° C) in summer. This cold desert can see frost and even snow. West of the Gobi is the Takla Makan Desert. Unlike the Gobi, the Takla Makan is covered with sand dunes. It is the world's largest shifting sands desert.

The vast grasslands of northern China make excellent pasture for grazing sheep and other animals.

In the Tibetan region of China is Mount Everest, the tallest mountain in the world. Its peak stands 29,035 feet (8,850 meters) above sea level. Only part of Mount Everest is in China. The other part is in Nepal. Mount Everest is part of the Himalayan mountain range, the tallest mountain range in the world. The Himalayas are not the only tall mountain range in China. The Karakoram mountain range runs north of the Himalayas. It is home to K2, the second tallest mountain in the world, at 28,251 feet (8,611 m). Like Mount Everest, only part of K2 is in China.

To the east, mountains give way to foothills. Most of China's farmland is in the eastern half of the country. In southern China, lush **subtropical** forests grow. A seasonal rain and wind known as a **monsoon** begins in southern China in early May. The Chinese call this rain *Meiyu*.

On May 29, 1953, Sir Edmund Hillary and Tenzing Norgay became the first people to climb Mount Everest. Since then, more than 3,000 people have made it to the top.

PLANTS AND ANIMALS

The diversity of China's animal and plant life is immense. The country has in excess of 6,200 species of **vertebrates** alone.

More than 100 animal species are found only in China. These include the South China tiger, the Chinese alligator, and the white-flag dolphin.

Climate and geography dictate what kinds of animals live where in China. The giant panda is China's best-known animal. These rare creatures have adapted to live in the bamboo forests of central China. Bactrian camels roam the Gobi and Takla Makan Deserts. Snow leopards, with their thick, warm fur, hunt in the high, cold mountains of the Himalayas. Golden snub-nosed monkeys swing through the mountain forests of southern China.

Plant life is also varied and abundant. Approximately 32,000 species of **higher plants** grow in China. Trees such as the Chinese cypress and the golden larch grow only in this country. The metasequoia, another tree native to China, is thought to be one of the oldest and most rare plants in the world. Needlegrass and gray sagebrush grow sparsely around the Gobi Desert. Lotus blossom and dove trees grow along the Yangtze River. Coconut palms offer shade to animals living in the tropical heat of Hainan Island.

The giant panda's furry body and seemingly huge black eyes give it appeal that crosses language and cultural barriers.

10% of the world's vertebrate species are found in China.

11 to 14 The number of hours a panda spends eating each day.

385 The approximate number of **threatened** species in China.

1,000 The number of different plant species used in traditional Chinese medicine.

10% Percentage of world's animal species found in China.

NATURAL RESOURCES

At least 171 different minerals can be found in China. They include titanium, zinc, and nickel, as well as rare earths, which are used to produce many high tech products. The Three Gorges Dam on the Yangtze River is the world's largest construction project. It can generate 22,500 **megawatts** of electricity. It also helps control flooding in the region.

With such a large population, food production in China is important. Farmland covers 540,000 square miles (1.4 million sq. km) of the country. These areas are used to produce crops, such as wheat and barley. Rice is China's most important crop. It is grown on 25 percent of the country's farmland.

China has about 27,000 square miles (71,000 sq. km) of freshwater lakes. Major lakes include Lake Poyang, which is China's largest. In addition to generating **hydroelectricity**, China's rivers are used for transportation and recreation.

95% The percentage of the world's rare earths China produces.

398 Tons China's gold production in 2011. (361 tonnes)

300 million The number of farmers in China.

5 trillion The number of gallons of water dammed by Three Gorges Dam. (19 trillion liters)

With more than half a million migratory birds, Lake Poyang is a favorite destination for birdwatchers.

TOURISM

After France and the United States, China is the most visited country in the world. A favorite destination is the Forbidden City in Beijing. Built between 1406 and 1420 AD, this palace complex is now a museum. In 1987, it was declared a **UNESCO** World Heritage site.

Perhaps the most famous tourist attraction in China is the Great Wall. The longest humanmade structure in the world, the wall is 13,172 miles (21,196 km) long. Construction of the wall began in the 3rd century BC. It was designed to stop invaders and control trade.

The Forbidden City covers more than 7.8 million square feet (725,000 sq. m) and consists of 980 buildings.

The Great Wall of China is 25 feet high (7.6 m) in some places and ranges from 15 to 30 feet wide (4.6 to 9.1 m).

One of the most extraordinary tourist attractions in China is the **Terracotta** Army. This archaeological site contains an estimated 6,000 life-size sculptures of soldiers, horses and other figures. Since the first sculptures were discovered in 1974, about 2,000 have been excavated. These figures represent the armies of Emperor Qin Shi Huang. Their purpose was to protect the emperor in the afterlife. They were buried with him in 210 BC. In 2012, a large palace was discovered near the Terracotta Army. It is believed this palace was meant to serve as the emperor's home in the afterlife.

Hainan Island, located off the southern coast of China, is also a popular destination for tourists. Sometimes called the "Hawai'i of the East," Hainan is home to many resorts. Its name means "south of the sea." Here, people can relax on the sandy beaches, play golf, or hike through lush, tropical rainforests. Most of the tourists who visit Hainan Island are from the Chinese mainland.

Tourism BY THE NUMBERS

58 MILLION

The number of tourists that visited China in 2011.

1.5X larger than Manhattan

The size of Mission Hills China, the largest golf course in the world.

1,000,000

Pieces of artwork contained in the Forbidden City.

Hainan is the smallest province in China, as well as the most southern. The province is comprised of Hainan Island and about 200 other smaller islands.

INDUSTRY

Since the 1950s, China's major industries have shifted away from farming and agriculture toward mining, manufacturing, construction, and power. China now has the world's second-largest economy, after the United States. It also has one of the fastest growing economies in the world.

In 1978, China began to move toward a more **free market** economy. Before that time, the government controlled industry. This shift towards **capitalism** meant companies could now sell their products to whomever they chose. Around the same time, many foreign companies began to move the production of their goods to Chinese factories. This work could be performed less expensively in China.

China is now one of the leading producers of consumer goods, including electronics and information technology products. The **textile** industry is another important aspect of the Chinese economy. Thousands of factories produce yarn, silk, and even synthetic fibers. China's other industries include clothing, footwear, toys, and food processing. These types of work are called light industry. Heavy industries in China include coal, iron, petroleum, and automobile manufacturing.

Energy remains one of the fastest growing industries in China. An abundant energy supply is required to fuel China's economic growth. Investment in alternative forms of energy, such as wind power, is an important part of China's energy program.

3.7 Billion tons
China's total coal consumption in 2011, the highest consumption in the world. (3.4 billion tonnes)

2009 The year China sold more automobiles than the United States.

10 million tons
The amount of coal China burns each day. (9 million tonnes)

#1 Consumer and producer of electricity in the world.

Women make up 46 percent of the Chinese workforce. Many of these women work in factories.

GOODS AND SERVICES

Goods and Services
BY THE NUMBERS

A low-cost work force and good **infrastructure** have helped make China one of the most productive countries in the world. China trades the goods it produces with many countries. Its top trading partners are the United States and the European Union, which includes France, Italy, Germany, Spain, and Sweden. Among China's top exports are electronics, medical equipment, and labor intensive products, such as clothing and shoes.

Food production in China has expanded greatly in recent years. China is now one of the world's largest food-producing nations. Tea is one of China's most important crops. It is sold all over the world. Also, almost one third of the world's salt is produced in China, making it the world's largest salt-producing nation.

1.18 BILLION
The number of mobile phones produced in China in 2012.

$784 MILLION
The value of the tea exported from China in 2010.

780 million
The number of people in China's workforce.

62 million tons
The amount of salt China produced in 2010.
(56 million tonnes)

China produces a wide variety of food crops, including sweet potatoes, wheat, corn, and sunflower seeds.

INDIGENOUS PEOPLES

A large number of **indigenous** groups live in China. Many of these groups are small and live in remote areas. The Akha people are from the southern Chinese province of Yunnan. They are a hill people. This means they live in hilly or mountainous regions, often at a distance from urban sites. In the late 1800s, the Akha began to move to parts of Thailand, Burma, and Laos.

The Lisu people are another hill tribe. They originated in the Tibetan region and later moved to Yunnan. Many of the people in these hill tribes became farmers and were among the first humans to cultivate rice.

The Manchu people are an indigenous group native to Manchuria, which is now a part of northeast China. Unlike some indigenous groups which are found only in specific areas, the Manchu are more widespread.

9,000 YEARS AGO
When the early inhabitants of China began to cultivate rice.

293 The number of languages spoken in China.

A headdress is a sign of social status for Akha women. Akha headdresses can be very ornate.

THE AGE OF EXPLORATION

1492 The year Christopher Columbus landed in America while trying to find a route to China.

4,000 miles The length of the Silk Road. (6,437 km)

54% The percentage of the world's silk produced by China.

Many people have explored China. One of the most important early Chinese explorers was Zhang Qian. In 138 BC, Qian was sent by the imperial court of the Han **dynasty** (206 BC–220 AD) to explore the western regions beyond its borders. Qian's explorations allowed the Han dynasty to increase trade with the people to the west. Qian is also credited with expanding the **Silk Road**, which was first established during the Han dynasty to allow the China's silk to be traded to Europe and Arabia. Qian is considered a national hero in China.

The desire to expand trade was a greatest motivator for exploration in China. The first Europeans to explore China were looking for ways to expand their trade routes. Among the earliest were the Radhanites. These Jewish merchants visited China as early as 500 AD.

One of the best-known Europeans to explore China was Marco Polo. Traveling with his father and uncle, Marco Polo left Italy and arrived in China between 1271 and 1275 AD. Over the next several years, Marco traveled throughout China. He studied the Chinese people, learned their customs, and enjoyed their culture. After he returned to Italy, Marco wrote about his travels. His book of adventures became popular throughout Europe.

Captured during a war with another city in Italy, Marco Polo wrote of his travels while in prison.

EARLY SETTLERS

The earliest settlers in China began to arrive during the Neolithic period, around 10,000 BC. These people settled in the valley regions around both the Yellow and the Yangtze Rivers. They were farmers and herders. Researchers suggest the origins of rice in China began in the valley of the Yangtze River about 9,000 years ago. Early settlers would have first collected wild rice before learning how to grow and cultivate it.

Around 3000 BC, the early Chinese built villages in the fertile basin of the Yellow River. One of the earliest cultures in China was the Longshan. They lived between 3000 and 2000 BC. Known for their highly polished black pottery, these people built the first cities in China.

Oracle bones contain the earliest evidence of writing in China.

The Zhou made beautiful objects out of bronze, many of which have survived to this day.

In 1928, archaeologists began to explore the ruins of Yin, the capital city of the Shang dynasty. The ruins included temples, palaces, and tombs. They also unearthed shells and bones inscribed with writing. Called oracle bones, the Shang would scratch questions onto them and then place them in fires to create cracks. These cracks would be interpreted as messages from **deities**. The discovery of these bones confirmed to the world that the Shang dynasty had been very advanced for its time.

The Shang dynasty lasted from 1600 BC to 1046 BC. At the Battle of Muye in 1046 BC, the Zhou dynasty defeated the Shang. The Zhou dynasty would go on to become the longest lasting dynasty in Chinese history. It ruled for more than 800 years.

Dynasties
BY THE NUMBERS

557 The total number of Chinese emperors.

2,132 The length of the imperial dynastic period in years.

1911 The year the last dynasty ended.

TEN The number of the major dynasties.

Steps, or terraces, are often cut into the sides of hills to allow farmers to grow more rice.

POPULATION

With almost 1.35 billion people, China is the most populated country in the world. Experts believe China's population will peak at 1.6 billion people by the year 2030. More than half of China's people live in cities, rather than in **rural** areas. Most of the population has settled along the eastern **seaboard** in large cities, such as Beijing and Shanghai.

As people seek better lives and greater opportunities, they often move from the countryside to the cities. There, many people have found work in China's many factories. This vast supply of workers has helped China to expand its economic power. It has also led to problems. With so many people moving to the cities, farming has suffered.

As the population of China grew, it began to put a strain on the country's resources and its ability to take care of all its citizens. Consequently, in 1979, China created the one-child policy to slow population growth. With few exceptions, families living in large cities were permitted to have only one child. Since its inception, it is estimated that the one-child policy has slowed the growth of the Chinese population by at least 100 million people.

104 million The population of the province of Guangdong.

12th largest in the world
What Guangdong would be if it were a country.

---

8 Million
The number of college and university graduates in China each year.

2025 The year China will have built enough skyscrapers to fill New York City 10 times over.

With most of the population living in urban areas, moving around a busy Chinese city can be a challenge.

POLITICS AND GOVERNMENT

I n the past, China was often ruled by dynasties. One of the best known is the Qin, which united China under one dynasty in 221 BC. Many other dynasties followed over the centuries. In 1911, however, China underwent a revolution, and the last imperial dynasty was removed from power. Today, the country is officially called the People's Republic of China. Its government is based on the values of **socialism** and **communism**. The Communist Party of China forms the government. It was founded in 1921.

China has been the source of much political and cultural debate. In 1989, students protested in what became known as the Tiananmen Square protests, from April 22 to June 4 in Beijing.

The citizens of some areas, such as Tibet and Taiwan, have had disputes with China over their independence. The Dalai Lama, for example, is an important religious and political leader from Tibet. He lives in exile and wishes to see Tibet become more independent. When the Communist Party of China took power in 1949, the previous government fled to Taiwan. To this day, Taiwan considers itself a separate country, though China claims it as a province.

250 The average number of protests held daily in China.

China has **22** provinces.

TWO
The number of special administrative regions. (Hong Kong and Macau)

82 Million

The number of members in the Communist Party of China.

Until 1997, Hong Kong was part of the British Empire. Although now part of China, it is considered a special administrative region and maintains a separate government system from the mainland.

CULTURAL GROUPS

China recognizes 56 distinct ethnic groups within the country. The largest ethnic group is the Han Chinese. Concentrated in the eastern half of China, the Han make up almost 92 percent of the Chinese population. Other ethnic groups include the Tibetan people of the Himalayan region and the Mongols in the far north.

There are many languages spoken in China. The most common is Mandarin, which is spoken by 70 percent of the population. It is the official language of the People's Republic of China. Other languages spoken in China include Wu, Cantonese, and Min.

Tibetan monasteries are often remote, providing Buddhist monks with peaceful surroundings for meditation, an important part of their belief system.

China's borders have shifted over the centuries. China is made up of many different cultural groups because of this. On occasion, areas once controlled by China have regained their independence. Mongolia was once a part of China, but became an independent country early in the 20th century.

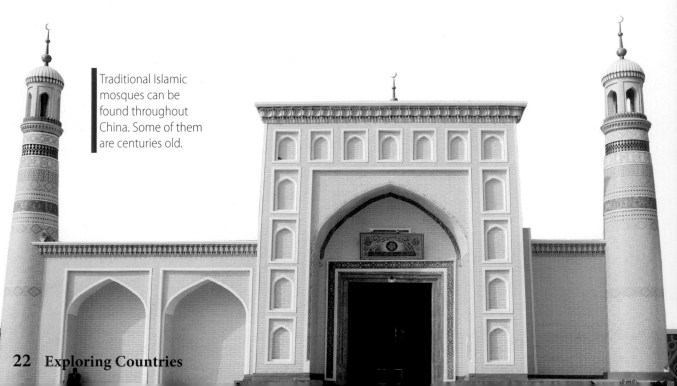

Traditional Islamic mosques can be found throughout China. Some of them are centuries old.

Even though Tibet is now a province of China, the people of Tibet have maintained their own customs and religions. This includes Tibetan Buddhism, which is different from the Buddhism practiced in other parts of China. Tibetan Buddhists often make journeys to remote monasteries as part of their religion.

China's major religions include Buddhism, Daoism, and Chinese folk religions. Chinese folk religions involve the worship of many deities. These deities include cultural heroes, ancestors, and even dragons. It is estimated that 50 percent of Chinese people practice some form of Chinese folk religion. Many Chinese combine different religions, creating a unique set of beliefs.

Buddhism is one of China's oldest religions. Although there are different forms of Buddhism, they all share a belief in **reincarnation**. Buddhists believe people are reborn after they die. Each person repeats the cycle of life and death until he or she becomes enlightened. Enlightenment is a spiritual state that is free from suffering. The religion is named after Buddha, the first person to achieve enlightenment. Merchants traveling the Silk Road brought Buddhism to China more than 2,000 years ago.

Cultural Groups BY THE NUMBERS

635 AD The year Persian Christians from the Middle East introduced Christianity to China.

2014 The Year of the Horse, according to Chinese astrology.

700 MILLION
The number of people who travel each year to visit family over Chinese New Year

Scholars believe Buddha was born in the 6th century BC. He lived around the same time as the ancient Greek philosophers Socrates and Plato.

ARTS AND ENTERTAINMENT

The arts have a very rich history in China. One of the oldest art forms in the world that is still practiced is Chinese painting. This ancient tradition involves detailed brushstrokes and uses black or colored inks and paint. Landscapes are a favorite theme. Chinese paintings can be found on hanging scrolls, pottery, and even folding screens.

Ming vases can be very expensive. In 2012, one sold for $1.3 million.

Sculpture dates back to the Stone Age in China. The life-size Terracotta warriors at the tomb of Emperor Qin Shi Huang were made in the third century BC. China also has a long history of sculptures carved from jade, a beautiful, green stone.

The Chinese are famous for their **porcelain**. During the dynastic period, skilled artists worked in large workshops. There, they created jars, bowls, and plates with intricate designs. Some of the most famous examples of Chinese porcelain were created during the Ming dynasty (1368-1644 AD).

The Terracotta warriors are believed to have been made by government workers and local artisans.

Sometimes called the "Father of all Chinese music," the qin is a string instrument. It is placed in the lap and played by plucking its strings. Older still is the Chinese sheng. Dating back to 1100 BC, this mouth organ has several vertical pipes. Another traditional instrument is the egg-shaped xun. It is a type of flute.

Chinese opera can be traced back to the third century BC. A combination of drama, music, dance, intricate makeup, and sets, Chinese opera is quite different from western opera. The singing in Chinese opera is often shrill and piercing. Loud drums and gongs are common. Martial arts and acrobatics are incorporated into the dancing. These operas were popular among the emperors of the past. Many of the same stories are still performed today.

$80 million
Most expensive vase ever sold, from the Qing dynasty.

2020 The year experts predict China will surpass the United States' film market.

The costumes of Chinese opera are very colorful and detailed.

SPORTS

Chinese interest in sport goes back thousands of years. There is evidence to suggest the Chinese were playing a form of soccer as early as 200 BC. Excellence in sports is a source of national pride, and physical fitness is an important part of daily life. Workers in factories and students in schools often participate in morning exercises. A great number of sports are popular in China, including martial arts, badminton, soccer, and swimming.

Sometimes called ping pong, table tennis is played by people of all ages in China.

People often practice a form of martial arts called Tai Chi in public, either alone or in groups.

Basketball is also popular. National Basketball Association (NBA) superstar Yao Ming is one of China's best-known athletes. The Houston Rockets drafted Ming in 2002. Before going to America, Ming played in the Chinese Basketball Association for five years, winning a championship in his final year. He was an NBA all-star eight times and reached the NBA playoffs four times with the Rockets.

China is known for its martial arts. Tai Chi is one of the country's most popular martial arts. It involves slow, relaxed movements, and is often practiced for its health benefits. Tai Chi has become very popular around the world. Wushu, sometimes called kung fu, is another Chinese martial art. It has been made famous in Hollywood films by movie stars such as Bruce Lee and Jackie Chan. The Buddhist monks of the Shaolin temple in the province of Henan have practiced their own form of wushu for centuries.

The Duanwu Festival, also known as the Dragon Boat Festival, is held every June. It is a national holiday in China. Throughout the country, teams race large dragon boats across lakes and rivers. Chinese dragon boat racing has become a popular sport around the world.

Sports BY THE NUMBERS

38 The number of gold medals China won at the 2012 summer Olympic games.

#2 China's ranking at the 2012 London Olympics.

300 MILLION
The estimated number of amateur table tennis players in China.

7 foot 6 inches: Height of NBA superstar Yao Ming, one of China's best-known athletes. (2.29 m)

China produces more than 60 percent of the world's bicycles. However, as cars have become more popular in China, bicycle use has declined.

Mapping China

We use many tools to interpret maps and to understand the locations of features such as cities, states, lakes, and rivers. The map below has many tools to help interpret information on the map of China.

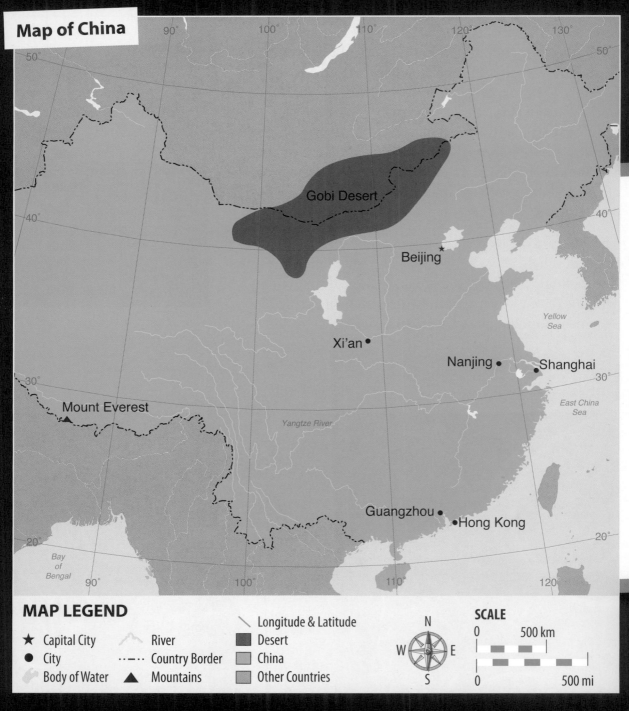

Map of China

Gobi Desert

Beijing ★

Yellow Sea

Xi'an ●

Nanjing ● ● Shanghai

Mount Everest ▲

East China Sea

Yangtze River

Guangzhou ● ●Hong Kong

Bay of Bengal

MAP LEGEND

★ Capital City	River	Longitude & Latitude
● City	Country Border	Desert
Body of Water	▲ Mountains	China
		Other Countries

SCALE

0 — 500 km

0 — 500 mi

N W E S

Mapping Tools

- The compass rose shows north, south, east, and west. The points in between represent northeast, northwest, southeast, and southwest.
- The map scale shows that the distances on a map represent much longer distances in real life. If you measure the distance between objects on a map, you can use the map scale to calculate the actual distance in miles or kilometers between those two points.

- The lines of latitude and longitude are long lines that appear on maps. The lines of latitude run east to west and measure how far north or south of the equator a place is located. The lines of longitude run north to south and measure how far east or west of the Prime Meridian a place is located. A location on a map can be found by using the two numbers where latitude and longitude meet. This number is called a coordinate and is written using degrees and direction. For example, the city of Los Angeles would be found at 34°N and 118°W on a map.

Map It!

Using the map and the appropriate tools, complete the activities below.

Locating with latitude and longitude
1. What city is located at 31° N and 121° E?
2. What desert is located at 45° N and 105° E?
3. What mountain is located at 27° N and 86° E?

Distances between points
4. Using the map scale and a ruler, calculate the approximate distance between Shanghai and Hong Kong.
5. Using the map scale and a ruler, calculate the approximate distance between Beijing and Xi'an.
6. Using the map scale and a ruler, calculate the approximate length of the Gobi Desert from its most eastern point to its most western point.

Quiz Time

Test your knowledge of China by answering these questions.

1 For which emperor was the Terracotta Army made?

2 What region of China is known as the "Roof of the World"?

3 What is the largest desert in Asia?

4 What is China's best-known animal?

5 What kind of energy does the Three Gorges Dam create?

6  How tall is Mount Everest?

7 What is China's most important crop?

8 What is the current population of China?

9 In what year did the Communist Party assume power in China?

10 Who is China's most famous basketball player?

ANSWERS
1. Qin Shi Huang
2. The Tibetan Plateau
3. The Gobi Desert
4. The giant panda
5. Hydroelectricity
6. 29,035 feet (8,850 m)
7. Rice
8. 1.35 billion people
9. 1949
10. Yao Ming

Key Words

capitalism: an economic system in which private owners control trade and industry for profit

communism: a system similar to socialism; does not believe in the idea of ownership of goods or property

deities: gods and goddesses; divine beings

dynasty: a succession of rulers from the same family line

free market: an economic system in which prices and wages are based on competition between businesses and government interference is limited

grasslands: large open areas of country covered by grass

higher plants: plants that have special tissues to move nutrients through their systems

hydroelectricity: electricity generated using water power

indigenous: native to a particular area

infrastructure: the basic elements, such as roads, bridges, and hospitals, needed for a society to function

megawatts: units of power equal to 1 million watts

monsoon: a strong, seasonal wind often accompanied by heavy rains

plateaus: broad, flat areas of high land

porcelain: a white ceramic that originated in China

reincarnation: rebirth after death into a new body

rural: areas away from cities

seaboard: the coastline

Silk Road: an ancient trading route that linked China with Europe and the Mediterranean Sea. It was named for the fact that Chinese silk was one of the most important products to travel it.

socialism: a social system based on shared ownership of a society's wealth

subtropical: a very humid and warm area near the equator

terracotta: a clay-based type of ceramic

textile: cloth or woven fabrics

UNESCO: the United Nations Educational, Scientific, and Cultural Organization. The aim of UNESCO is to promote world peace and the elimination of poverty through education, science, and culture.

vertebrates: animals that have backbones

Index

Akha 16
art 13, 24, 25

Beijing, China 7, 9, 12, 20, 21, 29
Buddhism 23

Christianity 22, 23
climate 4, 8, 9, 10
Communist Party 21, 30
cultural groups 22, 23

Dalai Lama 21
dance 25
deserts 4, 6, 7, 8, 9, 10, 29, 30
drama 25

food 11, 14, 15, 19
Forbidden City 12, 13
forests 4, 9, 10, 13

giant panda 5, 10, 30
Gobi Desert 6, 7, 8, 9, 10, 29, 30
grasslands 8
Great Wall of China 12

Hainan Island 10, 13
Himalayas 6, 9, 10, 22
Hong Kong 21

industry 14
Islam 22

languages 10, 16, 22
Lisu 16
Longshan 18

Manchu 16
martial arts 5, 25, 26, 27
minerals 11
monsoon 9
Mount Everest 9, 29, 30
music 25

petroleum 14
Polo, Marco 17
population 7, 11, 20, 22, 30

Qian, Zhang 17

rice 11, 16, 18, 19, 30
rivers 4, 6, 7, 10, 11, 18, 27, 28, 29

Shanghai 20, 29
Shaolin 27
Silk Road 17, 23
sports 26, 27

tea 15
Terracotta Army 13, 24, 30
Three Gorges Dam 11, 30
Tibet 9, 16, 21, 23
Tibetan Plateau 6, 30
tourism 12, 13

Yangtze River 6, 7, 10, 11, 18, 29

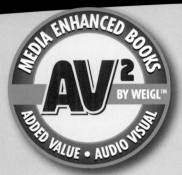

Log on to www.av2books.com

AV² by Weigl brings you media enhanced books that support active learning. Go to www.av2books.com, and enter the special code found on page 2 of this book. You will gain access to enriched and enhanced content that supplements and complements this book. Content includes video, audio, weblinks, quizzes, a slide show, and activities.

AV² Online Navigation

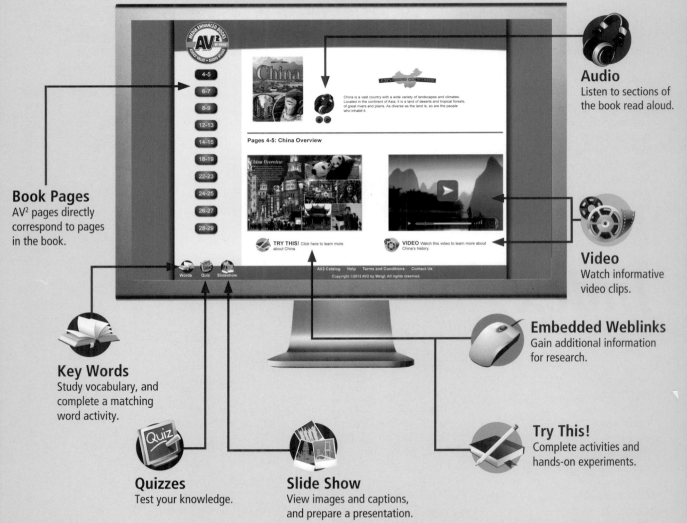

Audio
Listen to sections of the book read aloud.

Book Pages
AV² pages directly correspond to pages in the book.

Video
Watch informative video clips.

Key Words
Study vocabulary, and complete a matching word activity.

Embedded Weblinks
Gain additional information for research.

Try This!
Complete activities and hands-on experiments.

Quizzes
Test your knowledge.

Slide Show
View images and captions, and prepare a presentation.

AV² was built to bridge the gap between print and digital. We encourage you to tell us what you like and what you want to see in the future.

Sign up to be an AV² Ambassador at www.av2books.com/ambassador.

Due to the dynamic nature of the Internet, some of the URLs and activities provided as part of AV² by Weigl may have changed or ceased to exist. AV² by Weigl accepts no responsibility for any such changes. All media enhanced books are regularly monitored to update addresses and sites in a timely manner. Contact AV² by Weigl at 1-866-649-3445 or av2books@weigl.com with any questions, comments, or feedback.